Famous Faces from Norman Britain

Colouring Book

THUO BOOKS

Dedicated to my family

Copyright © 2025 Lucy Thuo All rights reserved.

No part of this book can be reproduced in any form or by written, electronic or mechanical, including photocopying, recording, or by any information retrieval system without written permission in writing by the author.

Published by Thuo Books

Printed by IngramSpark

ISBN: 978-1-73929-172-3

Although every precaution has been taken in the preparation of this book, the publisher and author assume no responsibility for errors or omissions. Neither is any liability assumed for damages resulting from the use of information contained herein.

Explore our full collection of enchanting colouring books at

www.thecolouringbook.co.uk

Edward the Confessor (1002/5-1066) was the son of Anglo-Saxon King Ethelred the Unready, who in 1016 died while England was being conquered by Danish King Canute the Great. After conquering England, Canute married Ethelred's widow, Emma of Normandy. Edward later succeeded Hardecanute, son of Canute and Emma, and became King of England. Edward's death in 1066 led to a succession crisis, as he had no children.

Edith of Wessex (c. 1025–1075) was the daughter of Godwin, the most powerful earl in England. She became the wife of Edward the Confessor. Her brothers included Harold Godwinson, who briefly became King, and Tostig, Earl of Northumbria.

Edward the Exile (1016-1057) was the son of King Edmund Ironside, who had been defeated by King Canute. Edward went into exile but when childless Edward the Confessor heard he was still alive, he was recalled and declared his heir. However, Edward the Exile died within days of arriving in England. His son Edgar Aetheling was elected as King by the King's Council in 1066 after Harold Godwinson died but he was never crowned and William the Conqueror became King instead.

Harold II, also called Harold Godwinson (c. 1020-1066), was the last crowned Anglo-Saxon king of England. He was son of a very powerful earl called Godwin and brother-in-law to Edward the Confessor. When Edward died with no heir, the King's Council chose Harold to succeed him. He was likely the first monarch to be crowned at Westminster Abbey. Harold's new position as King was not without opposition and, although he was successful in defeating Harald Hardrada's invasion in York, he was then defeated by William the Conqueror at the Battle of Hastings.

Harald Hardrada (1015-1066) was King of Norway. He invaded England in 1066 after unsuccessfully trying to conquer Denmark. He invaded England with Harold Godwinson's brother Tostig, who had been exiled. They were defeated by Harold Godwinson at the Battle of Stamford Bridge. Harald's death is often considered to mark the end of the Viking Age.

William I, also called William the Conqueror (c. 1028–1087), inherited the Duchy of Normandy from his father as a child but he found it hard to control and it took him decades to secure his position. In 1066 he invaded England and defeated Harold II at the Battle of Hastings. He became the first Norman king of England.

Matilda of Flanders (1031–1083) was the daughter of Count Baldwin V of Flanders and Adela of France, the sister of King Henry I of France. She married William the Conqueror and became Queen of England and Duchess of Normandy. She was mother to many children, including the kings William Rufus and Henry I.

According to some Norman sources, **Ivo Taillefer** was a jester who came with William the Conqueror to the Battle of Hastings. He juggled a sword and sang the Song of Roland at the enemy. An English soldier came to challenge him and Ivo won the fight before charging the English on his own. He was the first to attack in the Battle of Hastings. This picture is based on the illustration by Richard Caton Woodville Jr.

Hereward the Wake (flourished 1070–1071) was an Anglo-Saxon who led the local resistance against the Normans from his base on the Isle of Ely. Based on the picture by Patten Wilson.

Ralph de Gael (before 1042–c. 1110) was Earl of East Anglia. He wanted to marry Emma, the daughter of William FitzOsbern, 1st Earl of Hereford, who had been a great supporter of William the Conqueror and had been given vast amounts of land. William did not approve of the marriage between two such powerful families. However, they married without his blessing and were key people in the Revolt of the Earls in 1075. This picture is based on the illustration by Matilda Maria Blake.

Lanfranc (c. 1005–1089) was from Italy and had originally been a lawyer before becoming a Benedictine monk in Normandy. He was made Archbishop of Canterbury in 1070 after the Norman Conquest. In 1075 he helped William the Conqueror by detecting the Revolt of the Earls.

Odo (c. 1036–1097) was the half-brother of William the Conqueror and brother to Robert, Count of Mortain. He was made the Bishop of Bayeux by William. Both Odo and Robert fought with William at the Battle of Hastings. It is likely that Odo commissioned the Bayeux Tapestry.

Malcolm III Canmore, King of Scotland (c. 1031–1093), avenged his father Duncan I's death by seizing the Scottish throne from Macbeth. After the Norman Conquest, he gave refuge to the Anglo-Saxon Prince Edgar Aetheling and his sisters. He married Margaret, sister of Edgar Aetheling, as his second wife, his first having been Ingibiorg Finnsdottir, Harald Hardrada's niece.

William II, also called William Rufus (1056–1100), was the third (second surviving) son of William the Conqueror. He became King of England when William the Conqueror died, while the rule of Normandy was given to his older brother Robert. He died suspiciously while hunting and his younger brother Henry quickly became king in his place.

William de Warenne (died 1088) was one of the people that came with William the Conqueror to fight in the Battle of Hastings. He was hugely rewarded for his loyalty with land over 13 counties. He was later made Earl of Surrey by William Rufus.

Walter Tirel (1065–some time after 1100) was on a hunting trip in the New Forest with William Rufus when he fired an arrow that killed the King. It is debated whether it was accidental or planned. In panic, Walter fled to France. The King's body was taken to Winchester Cathedral.

Henry I (1069-1135) was the youngest son of William the Conqueror. He quickly became King after his brother William Rufus died on a hunting trip, while his elder brother Robert was returning from the First Crusade. He married Matilda of Scotland and they had two children: William Adelin and Matilda. Henry later married Adeliza of Louvain. The death of Henry's son William led to a succession crisis.

Matilda of Scotland, originally called Edith (1080-1118), was the first wife of Henry I. She was the daughter of the Scottish King Malcolm III and his wife, Margaret of Wessex. She was a descendant of the Anglo-Saxon kings, such as Alfred the Great and Edmund Ironside. By marrying a descendant of these kings, Henry I's legitimacy to rule was strengthened.

Anselm (1033/4–1109) was Archbishop of Canterbury from 1093 to 1109. He was exiled twice due to the Investiture Controversy, which was about whether church or monarch chose bishops. Anselm also proposed the ontological argument for God's existence.

Ranulf Flambard (c. 1060–1128) was keeper of the king's seal under William the Conqueror and William Rufus. He became William Rufus's chaplain, financial administrator and government minister, as well as Bishop of Durham. However, his fortune changed drastically on the death of William Rufus, as Henry I imprisoned him for embezzlement. Ranulf was the first person imprisoned in the Tower of London. It is said that he managed to escape through the window with a rope that had been smuggled into the tower in a barrel of wine. He went to Normandy and encouraged Robert Curthose to invade England.

Robert Curthose, Duke of Normandy (c. 1054–1134), was the eldest son of William the Conqueror. He inherited Normandy from his father but was unable to govern it well. One year after William Rufus died and Henry took over England, Robert invaded England but was unsuccessful. Henry later invaded Normandy and defeated Robert at the Battle of Tinchebrai. Robert became a prisoner for the rest of his life.

The Battle of Brémule happened on 20th August 1119. The fight was between Henry I of England and Louis VI of France. Louis VI supported the claim of William Clito, the son of Robert Curthose, to the Duchy of Normandy. However, Louis VI lost the battle and England stayed in control of Normandy.

The White Ship disaster happened on 25th November 1120. The ship sank, causing everyone on board (including William Adelin, who was the heir to the English throne and the only legitimate son of Henry I) to lose their lives, apart from a butcher called Berold. It was thought that William would have escaped but turned his escape boat back to try and help save his half-sister. The disaster led to the succession crisis called the Anarchy.

Adeliza of Louvain (c. 1103–1151) was the second wife of Henry I. She married Henry when she was about 18. She and Henry hoped to produce a male heir after the White Ship disaster but they did not have any children together. After Henry's death, Adeliza remarried and went on to have seven children with her second husband.

Adela of Normandy (c. 1067-1137) was the youngest daughter of William the Conqueror and Matilda of Flanders. She married Stephen II of Blois and one of their children was King Stephen of England.

King Stephen (c. 1097-1154) was the grandson of William the Conqueror through his mother Adela of Normandy and was the son of Stephen II, Count of Blois. He was married to Matilda I, Countess of Boulogne, a very capable queen consort. Stephen had almost been a passenger aboard the White Ship but changed his mind. After Henry I died, Stephen took the throne, leading to civil war against his cousin Matilda in what is known as the Anarchy.

Roger of Salisbury (died 1139) rose from being a priest of a chapel near Caen, Normandy, to being a hugely influential Lord Chancellor and Lord Keeper of England. He was also Bishop of Salisbury.

Empress Matilda (1102-1167) was the daughter of Henry I. Through her first marriage to Henry V of the Holy Roman Empire, she became an empress. She later married Geoffrey of Anjou. When her brother William died, she became Henry I's only legitimate heir. However, her cousin Stephen was crowned King instead, leading to civil war. Despite capturing Stephen, Matilda only ever became "Lady of the English". In a memorable incident, Matilda showed remarkable skills in escaping the besieged Oxford Castle on a snowy winter night, dressed in a white cape and rudimentary ice skates. Matilda's son Henry later became King Henry II.

Geoffrey Plantagenet, Count of Anjou (1113-1151), was the second husband of Empress Matilda. He became the father of Henry II, the first Angevin (named after Anjou) King of England. The name Plantagenet was a nickname given to Geoffrey, meaning broom shrub (planta genista), as he wore yellow broom flowers in his hat.

Robert, 1st Earl of Gloucester (c. 1090–1147), was the half-brother of Empress Matilda. He was her main military supporter during the Anarchy. He helped capture King Stephen at the Battle of Lincoln and imprisoned him at Bristol Castle. However, when Robert was captured at Stockbridge after the Rout of Winchester, he and Stephen were exchanged.

Henry of Blois (c. 1091–1171) was the grandson of William the Conqueror through his mother Adela of Normandy. He was the son of Stephen II, Count of Blois, and brother of King Stephen of England. Henry was Abbot of Glastonbury, Bishop of Winchester and papal legate. He was influential in resolving the Anarchy succession crisis with the Treaty of Wallingford in 1153, which proclaimed Matilda's son Henry as King Stephen's heir.

www.ingramcontent.com/pod-product-compliance
Lightning Source LLC
Chambersburg PA
CBHW042354070526
44585CB00028B/2926